ISBN: 9798735629757

Imprint: Independently published

Disclaimer: All answers are correct as of 30th April 2021.

The Professional Foul presents:

Manchester United Crossword

Check out our other books:

Liverpool Crossword
Arsenal Crossword
Chelsea Crossword
Manchester City Crossword
Tottenham Hotspur Crossword
Everton Crossword
Newcastle United Crossword
Leeds United Crossword
Celtic Crossword
Rangers Crossword
England Crossword

""I never wanted Manchester United to be second to anybody. Only the best would be good enough."

- Sir Matt Busby

"My greatest challenge is not what's happening at the moment. my greatest challenge was knocking Liverpool right off their f*****g perch. And you can print that."

- Sir Alex Ferguson

"I have always considered myself to be very fortunate. To play for the biggest club in the world. which also happens to be the team I supported as a boy. means I have never had to consider changing away from Manchester United."

Ryan Giggs

Contents Page

Round 1 - Founding & History

Manchester United Football Club was founded in 1878 and played their first recorded match in 1880. By 1950 they had achieved two league titles and two FA Cups to their name. This crossword covers the earliest decades of the club's history.

Across

3. In 1908 they became the first ever winners of this trophy (7,6)

6. Manager who led them to their first major trophy in 1908. (5,8)

7. They were banned from selling this in their stadium during the 1904/05 season.

11. 15-year-old discovered in Belfast by scout Bob Bishop whose telegram to the then manager read "I think I've found you a genius." (6,4)

12. The club's name when it was founded in 1878. (6,5)

14. In their first recorded match they lost 6-0 to the reserve team of this local side. (6,9)

16. Club captain who refused to play extra-time in an 1886 FA Cup tie against Fleetwood Rangers, leading to their elimination. (4,6)

17. Small Heath, who United defeated in a play-off game to retain their first division status in 1893 later became this Midlands side. (10,4)

18. Stadium that United played their "home" games at when their stadium was damaged during WWII (5,4).

19. Legendary manager appointed in October 1945. (4,5)

20. The club moved into this stadium in 1908.

Down

1. Chairman who saved the club from bankruptcy in 1927. (5,6)

2. Spanish side that knocked United out of their first ever European Cup campaign (4,6).

4. Scottish inside forward signed from Manchester City that was killed in WWI (5,8).

5. Team captain who found four businessmen to invest in the club, thus saving it from bankruptcy in 1902. (5,8)

8. After Manchester United refused to relinquish their union membership in 1909, they became known as "The _____".

9. Welsh winger, considered one of the early superstars of football and received man of the match in the 1906 FA Cup Final. (5,8)

10. Wealthy British brewery owner who was the first president of the newly named Manchester United. (4,5,6)

13. Merseyside rivals United lost to in the 1894 play-offs leading to relegation.

15. One of the new breed of managers who were retired players that took charge in 1932. (5,6)

Round 3 - Sir Matt Busby

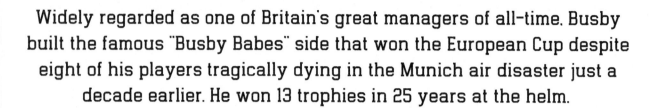

Widely regarded as one of Britain's great managers of all-time. Busby built the famous "Busby Babes" side that won the European Cup despite eight of his players tragically dying in the Munich air disaster just a decade earlier. He won 13 trophies in 25 years at the helm.

Across

1. National team he briefly managed in 1958.

6. Administrator and scout largely credited with bringing Busby to the club in 1945. (5.5)

9. Man that he handed over managerial duties to in 1969 following his retirement. (4.10)

10. 18-year-old centre-half signed by Busby who went on to make 688 appearances for the club. (4.7)

11. Opposition played in the European Cup match before the Munich air disaster. (3.4.8)

13. Closest Scottish Premiership club to his birth town in Lanarkshire.

16. His father was killed in the battle of ____ during WWI.

17. Busby successfully rebuilt his side and won the 1963 FA Cup Final against this team. (9.4)

18. His parents were both from this former Soviet state.

19. Spanish side that Busby turned down the opportunity to manage in 1956. (4.6)

Down

2. Scot signed by Busby in 1962 from Torino. (5.3)

3. Diminutive outside right signed from Birmingham City whose career was ended after the Munich air disaster at age 31. (6.5)

4. Opponents in the 1968 European Cup Final victory.

5. First English club he played for (10.4).

7. Future long-time assistant manager who he faced on his sole cap for Scotland in a match against Wales. (5.6)

8. Teenager. capped by England at 17 that Busby signed in 1952. judged to be one of the finest players of his era. (6.7)

10. Northumberland-born club legend signed in 1956. (5.8)

12. Goalkeeper throughout most of Busby's reign at United. (5.5)

14. Team he signed for as a player in 1936 and played for 9 years.

15. London side he made three appearances for as a player during WWII.

Round 2 - Old Trafford

Old Trafford has been United's home since 1910. It has gone through multiple upgrades and has seen many great moments over the decades and now boasts a capacity of 74,140. Can you answer these 20 questions about the red devils spiritual home?

Across

1. The club's south stand is now named after this club legend. (5.8)

4. Old Trafford has twice hosted the World Cup Final for this sport in 2000 and 2013. (5.6)

9. In March 2021. Manchester United women played their first game at Old Trafford against this London side. (4.3.6)

11. Stadium's nickname. (7.2.6)

13. Hosted a Euro 96 semi-final between France and this team. (5.8)

14. Colloquial name of the West Stand. (9.3)

15. The highest ever attendance at Old Trafford was a FA Cup semi-final between Wolverhampton Wanderers and this Lincolnshire side nicknamed "the Mariners". (7.4)

16. Name of the annual charity game between England and the Rest of the World. (6.3)

17. Name of the road Old Trafford is located on. (3.4.5.3)

18. Furthest Premier League stadium away from Old Trafford in the 2020/21 season.

19. Opponents in United's first ever match at Old Trafford in 1910.

Down

2. United's first game back at the stadium after its WWII bombing was against this local rival. (6.9)

3. Runners up in the only Champions League Final hosted there.

5. Name of the famous Scottish architect who designed Old Trafford as well as many other famous grounds around the UK. (9.6)

6. Brazil legend who opened the club museum in 1998.

7. Name of the report which suggested all First Division stadiums be converted into all-seaters.

8. Only stadium in the UK bigger than Old Trafford.

10. Name of the statue of Sir Bobby Charlton. Denis Law and George Best. (4.7)

12. Yorkshire victors of the "Khaki Cup Final" in 1915 hosted at Old Trafford.

14. Opponents in England's last international played at Old Trafford in 2007.

Round 4 - Sir Alex Ferguson

Sir Alex Ferguson is arguably the greatest manager in the sports history. The Scot won 38 trophies in his 26-year tenure (an all-time record) including 13 Premier League titles. 5 FA Cups and two Champions League's.

Across

1. Name of his horse that won the 2002 2000 Guineas at Newmarket. (4.2.9)

2. Nickname for Beckham. Scholes. Nicky Butt and the Neville brothers who came into the first team around the same time. Fergie's _____.

3. Team that his son Darren has managed on three separate spells.

4. His assistant from 2002-03 and 2004-08. (6.7)

10. Ferguson said in his autobiography that he was offered a £40.000 bribe to sell this Russian winger. (6.11)

14. Broadcaster he boycotted for seven years from 2004.

15. City which he completed the clubs first ever treble after defeating Bayern Munich.

16. Manager at United before his appointment in 1986. (3.8)

17. Club he managed before Aberdeen. (2.6)

18. Name of his assistant who arrived with him from Aberdeen. (6.4)

Down

1. Serbian side Ferguson defeated in the European Super Cup in 1991. (3.4.8)

4. Victory came against this London side in the 1990 FA Cup Final (7.6)

5. Former United player and Celtic manager that Ferguson had a feud with. which started after he agreed a move to FC Cologne without telling him whilst manager at Aberdeen. (6.8)

6. A hat trick from this player during a 5-5 draw denied Ferguson victory in his last ever game for Manchester United. (6.6)

7. Striker signed in 1992 having failed in an attempt to bring Alan Shearer and David Hirst to the club. (4.6)

8. City of birth.

9. He became the only British manager to win the Intercontinental Cup by beating this Brazilian side.

11. Before the start of the 2006/07 season this newspaper wrote an article about Ferguson titled "Shredding his legacy at every turn". (3.8)

12. Forward who scored the winner in a 1-0 FA Cup victory against Notts Forest which saved Ferguson's job. (4.6)

13. American university he took up a "long-term teaching position" at in 2014.

Round 5 - 1950/60s

This entire period was under the leadership of legendary manager Sir Matt Busby. Players including Sir Bobby Charlton. George Best and Denis Law graced the Old Trafford pitch. 5 First Divisions. a FA Cup and European Cup were won during these two decades.

Across

1. Defender who could play in midfield and up front who is currently secretary of the United Former Players' Association. (5.6)

4. Scottish midfielder signed from Celtic who said. "Where I was brought up. you had to be able to run or fight. and you know about my running". (3.7)

6. Scored a brace in the 1963 FA Cup Final victory over Leicester City. (5.4)

9. Player signed in 1953 for £29.999 as Busby didn't want him to burden being a £30,000 player. (5.6)

10. Full-back that won 33 caps for England and died in the Munich air disaster. (5.5)

12. European giant that ended United's European Cup defence in 1969.

13. Northern Ireland international who survived the air disaster but was forced to retire aged 24. (6.12)

16. England World Cup winning midfielder who made 395 appearances for the club from 1960-71. (5.6)

18. 19-year-old who scored in the 1968 European Cup Final. (5.4)

19. Midlands team that defeated them in the 1957 FA Cup Final. (5.5)

20. Centre forward who led the line for Benfica in the 1968 European Cup Final.

Down

2. The last league game played before the Munich air disaster was a 6-3 victory against this London side.

3. Argentine side United defeated in the 1968 Intercontinental Cup.

5. Club legend who retired in 1953 and was the first Irish player to win a trophy with United. (6.5)

7. Italian club defeated in the semi-finals of the 1968 European Cup.

8. North West team that defeated them in the 1958 FA Cup Final. (6.9)

11. The youngest victim of the Munich air disaster. (5.6)

14. Nationality of Carlo Sartori who joined the club in 1965 and became one of the first non-British or Irish players to come through United's youth ranks.

15. Northern Irishman considered one of the greatest in the history of the sport. (6.4)

17. Irish left-back who played in the European Cup final despite rupturing his achilles tendon in the quarters. (4.5)

Round 6 - 1970/80s

An unsuccessful era for United which included a relegation in 1974. There were three FA Cup victories but no first division titles. The end of this era saw the appointment of a certain Scotsman called Alex Ferguson.

Across

5. Atlantic Island where Sir Alex made his only first team appearance for United.

6. Spanish side that United beat in the 1983/84 Cup Winners' Cup quarter-final.

8. Third Division Dorset side that knocked United out of the FA Cup in 1984.

10. South coast team defeated in the 1983 FA Cup Final after a replay. (8.3.4.6)

12. Scored the sole goal in the 1985 FA Cup Final victory over Everton. (6.9)

14. Striker who was given a free transfer in 1973 to Manchester City who would then score against United to confirm their relegation in that season. (5.3)

16. Irishman appointed boss in 1971. (5.8)

17. First English-born Republic of Ireland international and popular figure who was the first member of the 1968 European Cup winning side to pass away. (4.7)

18. Appointed manager in November 1986. (4.8)

19. England international signed from Chelsea in 1979 who went on to make 194 appearances for the club. (3.7)

Down

1. Arsenal player who scored the winner in the classic 1979 FA Cup Final after the United had battled back from 2-0 down. (4.10)

2. Long-serving Scottish midfielder whose goal clinched United's promotion back to the first division in 1975. (3.6)

3. Manager commonly known as "The Doc" who was appointed in 1972. (5.8)

4. Scottish centre-back signed for a club record £120,000 in 1972. (6.6)

5. Club that Mark Hughes was re-signed from.

7. Danish winger signed from Ajax in 1984. (6.5)

9. Newly promoted London side playing First Division football for the first time since the 1950s that beat United in a shock result in 1986. (8.8)

11. Midfielder signed for a British record £1.5 million from West Brom and was appointed as United's global ambassador in 2008. (5.6)

13. Manager brought in from QPR in 1977 and would last four seasons. (4.6)

15. Team that United prevented from completing the treble by winning the 1977 FA Cup final.

Round 7 - 1990s

United were back to their very best during this decade as they dethroned archrivals Liverpool. The new Premier League era brought back the good times as the club achieved 5 league titles 3 FA Cups and an unprecedented treble to finish the decade in 1999.

Across

2. Midfielder signed for a British record £3.75 million in 1993. (3.5)

3. Host stadium of the 1999 Champions League Final. (3.4)

7. Player who went the other way when Andy Cole signed from Newcastle. (5.9)

8. Side that won the last ever First Division trophy at United's expense in 1992.

9. Dutch host city of the 1991 Cup Winners' Cup Final defeat at the hands of Barcelona.

10. Long-serving Welsh utility player released at the end of the 1993/94 season.

14. Stadium where Ryan Giggs scored his legendary FA Cup semi-final replay goal against Arsenal in 1999. (5.4)

16. Former manager who passed away in January 1994. (4.5)

18. Irish left-back who made 529 appearances for United from 1990-2002. (6.5)

19. Frenchman signed from Leeds in 1992. (4.7)

Down

1. Third highest goalscorer in Premier League history. signed in 1995. (4.4)

3. Team defeated in the 1999 FA Cup Final.

4. Fellow Greater Manchester side defeated in the 1993/94 FA Cup semi-final after a replay. (6.8)

5. Scored a late brace against Sheffield Wednesday to clinch the inaugural Premier League title. (5.5)

6. Stadium where the infamous "kung-fu" incident took place. (8.4)

11. Goalkeeper who conceded David Beckham's famous halfway line strike in 1996. (4.8)

12. Scored Bayern's goal in the 1999 Champions League Final. (5.6)

13. Team defeated 4-0 in the 1994 FA Cup Final to complete the club's first ever double.

15. Centre-back signed from Blackburn Rovers in 1994 for £1.2 million and stayed at the club until 2003. (5.3)

17. Club that legendary goalkeeper Peter Schmeichel was signed from.

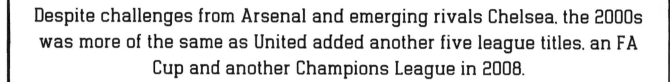

Despite challenges from Arsenal and emerging rivals Chelsea. the 2000s was more of the same as United added another five league titles. an FA Cup and another Champions League in 2008.

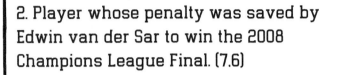

Across

2. Player whose penalty was saved by Edwin van der Sar to win the 2008 Champions League Final. (7,6)

3. FA Cup final opponents in 2004.

7. Club that Dwight Yorke joined in 2002 from United. (9,6)

8. Edwin van Der Sar and Louis Saha were both signed from this club.

9. The major signing of 2002. (3,9)

12. First Korean player to play for the club. (4,2,4)

13. Top goalscorer in three consecutive seasons from 2001-2004. (4,3,10)

14. French World Cup and European Championship winning goalkeeper signed in 2000. (6,7)

17. The only player to play for England having not lived in the UK. (4,10)

19. Man of the match in the 2009 League Cup Final triumph against Spurs. (3,6)

20. South American side defeated in the 2008 FIFA Club World Cup Final. (3,5)

Down

1. Swedish striker signed on loan in 2007. (6,7)

4. Assigned the number 7 shirt when Cristiano Ronaldo was sold to Real Madrid. (7,8)

5. Top goalscorer in the 2000/01 season. (5,10)

6. Became the first player to move between the two Manchester Clubs since 1999. (6,5)

10. Club that 18-year-old Cristiano Ronaldo was signed from in 2003. (8,2)

11. French defender who started the comeback from 3-0 down against Spurs to win 5-3 in 2001. (7,5)

15. Twin full-backs Fábio and Rafael da Silva were signed from Rio based side Fluminense. Which local rivals did the brothers actually support?

16. Defender sold to Lazio which Ferguson later described as "an error". (4,4)

18. Brazilian who scored a stunning hat trick at Old Trafford and was given a standing ovation in 2003.

Round 9 - 2010s

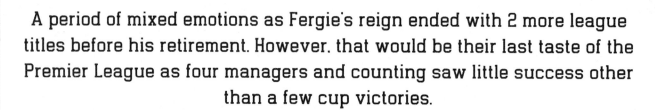

A period of mixed emotions as Fergie's reign ended with 2 more league titles before his retirement. However, that would be their last taste of the Premier League as four managers and counting saw little success other than a few cup victories.

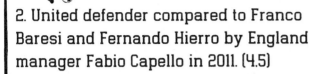

Across	Down

Across

2. United defender compared to Franco Baresi and Fernando Hierro by England manager Fabio Capello in 2011. (4.5)

4. Club that Daley Blind was signed from and sold to.

6. Tyneside-born midfielder who retired in 2018 after 464 appearances for the club. (7.7)

7. First Japanese player to play for the club. (6.6)

8. Meaning "little pea" in Spanish. what did Javier Hernández have printed on the back of his shirt?

14. Armenian used in the deal that brought Alexis Sanchez to the club.

18. Frenchman who scored on his debut against Liverpool in 2015. (7.7)

19. Robin van Persie scored a hat trick including a stunning volley from a Wayne Rooney pass against this club in 2013. (5.5)

20. Marcus Rashford scored a brace on his Manchester United debut against this Danish side.

Down

1. Spanish side defeated at the semi-final stage in United's 2016/17 Europa League winning campaign. (5.4)

3. Scored a hat trick against Liverpool in September 2010. (7.8)

5. Club that Ander Herrera was signed from in 2014. (8.6)

9. Team that Louis van Gaal defeated in the 2016 FA Cup Final. his only trophy at the club. (7.6)

10. Team defeated in the Champions League last 16 having lost the first leg 2-0 in 2014.

11. Ivorian signed from Villareal in 2016. (4.6)

12. Scored Barcelona's second goal and received man of the match in the 2011 Champions League Final. (6.5)

13. Played his first game back from retirement in a FA Cup tie against Manchester City. (4.7)

15. Side defeated in the 2017 League Cup Final.

16. Goalkeeper signed in 2011 from Atlético Madrid. (5.2.3)

17. Host city of the 2017 Europa League Final.

Round 11 - Ole Gunnar Solskjær

OGS' most famous moment in a United shirt came when he scored the winning goal in the 1999 Champions League Final to secure an unprecedented treble. He took over as manager in 2019 hoping to bring the glory days back to Old Trafford.

Across

3. Lancashire team he made his debut against. (9.6)

6. Whilst playing for the national team he formed a formidable partnership with this former Chelsea striker. (4.5.3)

7. Spanish opposition for his testimonial game in 2008.

9. Commonly nicknamed the baby-faced _____.

10. Took the corner in the build-up to his winning goal in the 1999 Champions League Final. (5.7)

12. United were the first team in the history of the European Cup to advance after losing the first leg at home by two goals or more against this side in 2019. (5.5.7)

13. He retired at the age of 34 due to a _____ injury.

18. He scored four goals off the bench (a Premier League record) against this club in 1999. (10.6)

19. National team he was invited to manage in 2009.

20. Club he supported as a child.

Down

1. Name of his daughter who plays in the MUWFC academy.

2. Club that United signed him from in 1996.

4. OGS started both 1996/97 Champions League semi-final legs which United lost to the eventual winners _____. (8.8)

5. Manager he took over from at United. (4.8)

8. United accepted an offer of £5.5 million for Ole in 1998 from this London Club. (9.7)

11. His first club.

14. Man he appointed assistant manager in 2019. (4.6)

15. Club he managed briefly in 2014. (7.4)

16. His last match as a player for United was the 2007 FA Cup Final against this side.

17. He became the first United manager to win his first four games since _____. (4.5)

Round 10 - Wayne Rooney

This round is all about the club's all-time leading goalscorer and one of the greats. Rooney scored 253 goals in 559 games after he signed from Everton as an 18-year-old. He won 5 Premier Leagues. a FA Cup and Champions League during his 13 seasons at Old Trafford.

Across

1. His last United game was against this Dutch opposition.

2. Club he scored a winner against on the final day of the 2011/12 season.

6. Rooney was United's most expensive teenager until this player signed in 2014. The record was broken again in 2015 by the signing of Anthony Martial. (4.4)

7. Name of his reality TV show broadcast on Sky from 2008-2010. (6.7)

10. Name of his wife who he met at school.

11. Only player who has scored more Premier League goals than Rooney. (4.7)

12. Player who had the number 10 shirt before him. (4.3.10)

13. Club he scored from almost 60 yards against in 2014 with David Beckham watching in the stands. (4.3.6)

15. Greater Manchester club he scored his 100th United goal against. (5.8)

19. Club he scored a hat-trick against in an 8-2 win (the first of which being his 150th United goal).

Down

1. Team he won his first England cap against.

3. Club he was appointed manager of in 2020. (5.6)

4. Club he scored a hat trick against on his United debut.

5. National team he rejected an approach from at the age of 16. (8.2.7)

8. Religion he was brought up under. (5.8)

9. Man he overtook to become United's and England's all-time top goalscorer. (5.8)

14. MLS club he played two seasons for. (2.6)

16. Club that Everton preferred Rooney to join instead of United in order to get a bigger transfer fee.

17. Player whose deflected cross set up his incredible bicycle kick goal in the Manchester derby.

18. Stadium he described as the hardest test and said "I never enjoyed playing there"

Round 12 - Class of '92

A golden generation of United youth players who came through in the early 1990s that went on to achieve great success for the club over the next two decades.

Across

1. Club owned by David Beckham that appointed Phil Neville as manager in 2021. (5.5)

6. Football league club that the six of them have part owned since 2014. (7.4)

7. Player who Zinedine Zidane described as his toughest opponent. (4.7)

9. Paul Scholes became the first player to score against both Inter Milan and AC Milan at the San Siro in the Champions League. The official name of the stadium is the Stadio _____. (8.6)

11. Nicky Butt started the 1999 Champions League Final as this midfielder was suspended. (3.5)

13. Club that Beckham was loaned to in 1994. (7.5.3)

14. Greater Manchester town that the Neville brothers were born in.

16. Second member of the six to leave the club. (5.4)

17. Player who Sir Alex hurled a boot at, causing a cut and requiring stitches. (5.7)

19. Paul Scholes scored a stunning long-range winner in a 2008 Champions League semi-final tie against this opposition.

20. Welsh midfielder who was part of the 1991/92 FA Youth Cup winning squad. He went on to play for Leicester City and Blackburn Rovers among others. (6.6)

Down

2. The Neville brothers' father's first name.

3. Manager of the youth team from 1981-2008 credited with raising the Class of '92. (4.8)

4. Went on to manage the England women's team. (4.7)

5. Club that Ryan Giggs spent part of his youth career at before signing for United. (10.4)

8. Match of the Day pundit who famously said about United "you'll never win anything with kids". (4.6)

10. Club United played in a friendly match to mark the 20th anniversary of the 1999 treble in which Beckham. Scholes. Butt and Gary Neville featured. (6.6)

12. Team that United beat in the 1991/92 FA Youth Cup Final. (7.6)

15. United's all-time record appearance holder. (4.5)

18. Gary Neville's final United goal came against this Champions League opposition in Fergie's 1000th game as manager.

Round 13 - Academy Graduates

The Manchester United academy is renowned around the world for producing great talents. Can you name this select group of 20 players?

Across

1. Won 80 caps for Scotland and also played for West Brom and Stoke. (6.8)

3. Belgian international of Albanian descent who scored a brace on his first league start for the club away at Sunderland. (5.7)

10. Manchester-born forward sold to Arsenal for £16 million by Louis van Gaal. (5.7)

12. England international who signed for Everton in a £30 million deal in 2017. (7.5)

14. Scored an injury time winner on his debut against Aston Villa after a turn and curling finish from the edge of the box. (8.7)

17. Frenchman who returned to the club from Juventus for a then world record £89.3 million. (4.5)

18. Scored 17 goals in his breakthrough 2019/20 season. (5.9)

19. Brazilian right back signed as a 17-year-old.

20. Player who the following Sir Alex quote is about: "A brilliant footballer. Brilliant ability. Top class ability. Needs to get away from Manchester and start a new life". (5.8)

Down

2. Scored over 100 career goals in the Premier League and Championship and is a member of the England one cap club. (7.8)

4. Right-back who won the title with Leicester in 2016. (5.7)

5. Made 79 appearances for United before going on to play for Everton and Watford among others. (3.9)

6. England international who has been out on 5 loan spells since turning professional in 2011. (5.7)

7. Stoke City's all-time record appearance holder. (4.9)

8. Irish international who scored the winner against Italy at Euro 2016.

9. Awarded an MBE for his campaigns on homelessness and child hunger. (6.8)

11. Lancaster-born Scottish international midfielder who grew 14 inches in two years whilst in the youth academy. (5.9)

13. Right-back who knocked out Wayne Rooney whilst sparring in a kitchen in 2017. (4.8)

15. Belfast-born centre-back who made 198 appearances for the club between 2006-2015. (5.5)

16. Oslo-born forward who has played Premier League football for Bournemouth and Everton. (4.4)

Round 14 - Club Captains

The club have had many legendary captains in their history. Can you name the last 20 based on their years as captain as well as the number of appearances and goals for the club?

Across

3. 1959-60 - 294 apps. 178 goals (6.7)

6. 1996-97 - 185 apps. 92 goals (4.7)

7. 1982 - 194 apps. 10 goals (3.7)

10. 1973 - 46 apps. 2 goals (6.6)

11. 2017-18 - 464 apps. 24 goals (7.7)

13. 2018-19 - 339 apps. 25 goals (7.8)

14. 2005-11 - 602 apps. 7 goals (4.7)

17. 1962-64 - 146 apps. 8 goals (4.8)

18. 1982-94 - 461 apps. 99 goals (5.6)

19. 1967-73 - 758 apps. 249 goals (5.8)

20. 1964-67 - 454 apps. 262 goals (5.3)

Down

1. 2011-14 - 300 apps. 21 goals (7.5)

2. 1994-96 - 414 apps. 51 goals (5.5)

4. 1997-05 - 480 apps. 51 goals (3.5)

5. 2019-present - 107 apps. 5 goals and counting (5.7)

8. 2014-17 - 559 apps. 253 goals (5.6)

9. 1960-62 - 192 apps. 14 goals (7.7)

12. 1975-82 - 456 apps. 4 goals (6.6)

15. 2019 - 261 apps. 19 goals (6.5)

16. 1973-75 - 296 apps. 34 goals (6.6)

Round 15 - Cristiano Ronaldo

Despite only spending six seasons at Old Trafford, Cristiano Ronaldo could be considered a club icon. The 2008 Ballon d"Or winner won three Premier League titles and a Champions League after arriving as an 18-year-old in 2003.

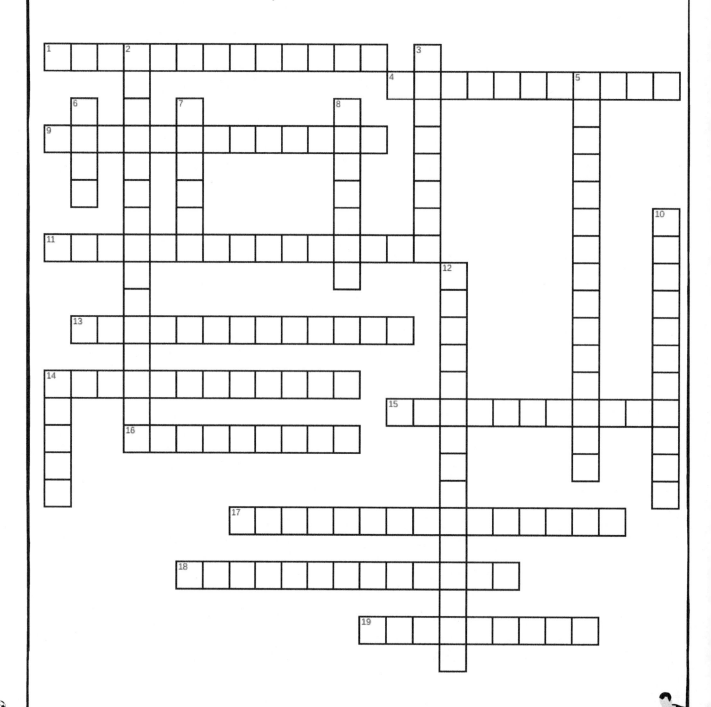

Across

3. He became the first United player to win the Ballon d'Or since this player. (6.4)

4. He won the inaugural FIFA Puskás Award in 2009 with a 40-yard screamer against this opposition.

5. Atlantic island he was born on.

8. His final United goal was a free kick against this local rival. (10.4)

9. Wore the number 7 shirt at United before him. (5.7)

12. Sir Alex was quick to move for the 18-year-old after a friendly match at the inauguration of this stadium. (7.4.8)

15. An infamous incident in the 2006 World Cup quarter-final led to the sending off of this teammate. (5.6)

16. He scored the opening goal in the 2004 FA Cup Final against this team.

18. He scored his one and only United hat trick against this club.

19. Player he finished runner-up to in the 2007 Ballon d'Or.

Down

1. Club he made his United debut against. (6.9)

2. He holds the Champions League record for most goals against the same club. Which club?

6. His nationality.

7. His final game for Real Madrid came against this English side.

8. He scored United's 1000th Premier League goal in a 4-1 away defeat to this club in 2005.

10. He scored a stunning knuckleball free kick against Portsmouth in 2008 past this goalkeeper. (5.5)

11. It took him 30 games to score a Champions League goal. it eventually came in 2007 in a 7-1 win against this club.

13. The squad number he requested when he joined United but was instead given the number 7. (6.5)

14. Side he scored his first United goal against.

17. CR7 was the second player to reach the 100 international goals milestone. Who was the first? (3.4)

Round 16 - Roy Keane

Former club captain Keane appeared 480 times over a trophy laden 13 seasons. He captained United to their 1999 treble winning season and added a further six Premier League titles and four FA Cups.

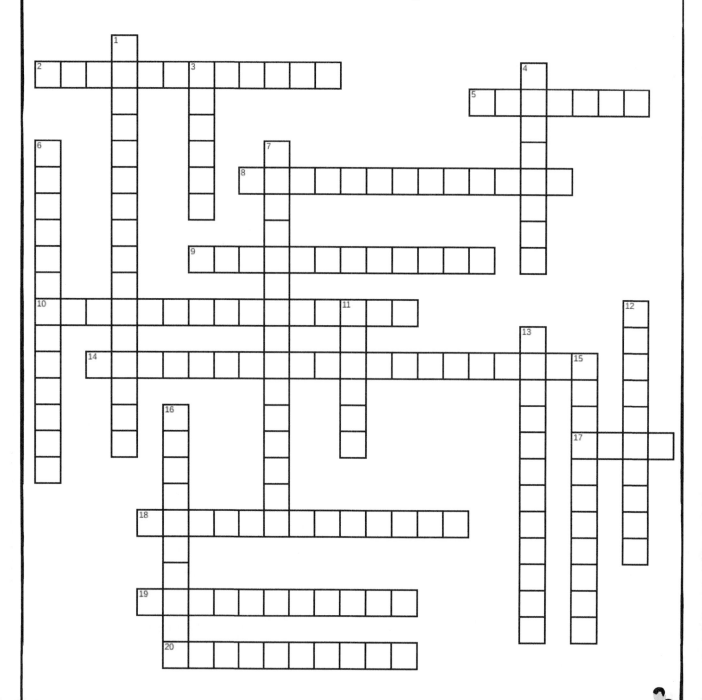

Across

2. In August 2002. Keane was fined £150,000 by Sir Alex and suspended for three matches for elbowing this Sunderland player. (5.7)

5. His middle name.

8. Norwegian he took revenge on in 2001 after an incident four years earlier that angered Keane. (3.4.6)

9. Ireland manager he had a public bust up with leading to his expulsion from the 2002 Ireland World Cup Squad. (4.8)

10. He scored twice on his Old Trafford debut against this Yorkshire club. (9.6)

14. Term coined after Keane criticized United fans after a game against Dynamo Kiev that describes fans who attend games that don't have an interest in football. (5.8.7)

17. City of birth.

18. United assistant manager he had a strained relationship with after he questioned Keane's loyalty. (6.7)

19. His last United goal came in March 2005 in a FA Cup tie against this south coast opposition.

20. His last United game ended in injury after a challenge from this Liverpool player. (4.6)

Down

1. Club United signed him from. (10.6)

3. Club he finished his career with and supported as a child.

4. His performance against this team was described by Sir Alex as "the most emphatic display of selflessness I have seen on a football field". arguably Keane's finest hour.

6. In a 2005 interview he criticised four teammates after a 4-1 defeat against this club.

7. Club that United stole the signature of Keane from after they didn't have the correct paperwork to complete the transfer. (9.6)

11. Name of his Labrador Retriever. described as the famous dog in football since Pickles.

12. His first management job. where he signed former United teammates Dwight Yorke and Liam Millar and led them to promotion.

13. Former Arsenal captain he maintained a fierce rivalry which culminated in the infamous tunnel altercation in 2005. (7.5)

15. In the 1999/00 season he became the first United player to win the PFA Men's Players' Player of the Year since this player. (4.7)

16. Referee involved in the 2005 tunnel incident away at Arsenal who later said he should have sent both players off. (6.4)

One of the Premier League's great central defensive partnerships. Rio and Vidić won five Premier League titles as well as a Champions League in seven seasons.

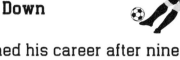

Across	Down

Across

2. South London district Ferdinand was born in.

4. Vidić is one of only three players to win the Premier League Player of the Season award twice alongside Thierry Henry and this former United player. (9.7)

5. Name of Ferdinand's cousin who is a former QPR. Spurs and England Striker.

7. Club that Ferdinand played in goal against in 2008 after an injury to Edwin van der Sar and a Tomasz Kuszczak red card.

12. Italian side that United hijacked Vidić's transfer from in 2005.

14. Club that Ferdinand finished his career at after the expiration of his United contract. (6.4.7)

15. Player that Ferdinand lifted the 2008 Champions League Trophy with. (4.5)

16. On 22nd January 2006. Ferdinand scored the winner for United at this stadium.

17. Club United signed Vidić from. (7.6)

18. Ferdinand scored the final Old Trafford goal of the Sir Alex Ferguson era against this side. (7.4)

19. Vidić received three standing ovations in his final game for the club on the 6th of May 2014 against this side. (4.4)

Down

1. Club Vidić finished his career after nine seasons at United. (5.5)

2. London club that Ferdinand was booed by United fans against in 2005 after he had yet to agree a new contract. (8.8)

3. Ferdinand became the world's most expensive defender for the second time when he signed for United. This Frenchman took his title the first time. (7.6)

6. Ghanaian who scored a penalty against Ferdinand during his only stint in goal for United. (6.7)

8. Vidić received a medal for his 2006 League Cup Final substitute appearances however he gave it to this teammate instead after his contributions in earlier rounds. (8.5)

9. Vidić scored United's 1000th Premier League goal at Old Trafford against this opponent. (9.7)

10. Club that Vidić was sent off in three consecutive appearances against and four times overall. a Premier League record for red cards against one team.

11. In 2008. Ferdinand completed 90 minutes and had three stitches in his foot at half time during a Champions League tie against this club.

13. Vidic's national team.

Round 18 - General I

You've done well to reach this point: I hope you have learnt lots of cool facts. Here are three rounds of general questions from a range of categories to finish off. Good luck!

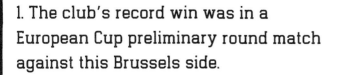

Across

1. The club's record win was in a European Cup preliminary round match against this Brussels side.

4. Club that Bruno Fernandes played for before Sporting Lisbon.

7. Australian re-signed as the predecessor to Peter Schmeichel. (4,7)

8. Second top goalscorer in the 2002/03 season behind Ruud van Nistelrooy. (4,7)

11. Team that defeated United 5-0 in the 1999/00 season (one of only three league defeats in that title winning season).

13. Argentine signed for a British record £28.1 million from Lazio in 2001. (4,9,5)

15. Kit manufacturer from 1992-2002.

16. The club's honorary president. (6,7)

17. Nigerian signed on loan from Shanghai Shenhua in 2020. (5,6)

18. Cork-born club legend signed from Oldham Athletic and spent 12 years at the club. (5,5)

19. Shirt sponsor from the 2021/22 season.

Down

1. Ivorian signed from Atlanta in 2021. (4,6)

2. Their record win in the FA Cup was 8-0 in 1964 against this West Country side. (6,4)

3. Winger signed from Torquay United in 1988 for £200,000 who went on to score 36 goals in 265 games for United. (3,6)

5. Scored his first goal at Old Trafford, in the sixth minute of stoppage time against local rivals Manchester City to give United a 4-3 derby win. (7,4)

6. The second highest transfer fee ever received by the club was for this player. (6,6)

9. Club that Fred was signed from. (8,7)

10. Number 21 for the 2020/21 season. (6,5)

12. Player who scored a brace at Anfield on 1st December 2002. (5,6)

14. United's first £1 million plus player who was signed from Nottingham Forest. (5,7)

Round 19 - General II

Across

1. Winner of the 2019-20 Denzil Haroun Reserve Team Player of the Year award. (5.6)

3. Goalkeeper when United won their first European Cup in 1968 and made 539 appearances for the club. (4.7)

6. Man of the match and goalscorer that secured United's first ever League Cup in 1992. (5.7)

8. Brazilian midfielder who is the only player to have won the Copa América whilst being a United player.

14. Home ground of the Manchester United Women's team. (5.6.7)

15. Signing in 1962 that was the first time United had broken the British transfer record and the first six-figure player. (5.3)

16. The only foreign player to have won the World Cup as a United player. (4.5)

19. Club that beat United 5-4 in a 4th round League cup tie in 2012.

Down

2. Liverpudlian winger who holds the record for the most consecutive appearances for an outfield United player (207 from 1977 to 1981). (5.7)

4. Russian airline that is United's official carrier.

5. Most appearances for an Irishman. (4.5)

6. Fourth on the list of all-time record appearances for the club. (4.7)

7. Dutch left-back that made 28 appearances and was sold to Dynamo Moscow in 2014. (9.7)

9. Scored the winner for United in the 1977 FA Cup final victory over Liverpool. (5.9)

10. The shortest ever appearance on the pitch for United was 11 seconds by this centre-back against Norwich City in 2012. (5.8)

11. Chelsea manager who sold Juan Mata to United in January 2014. (4.8)

12. Manager who won United's 12th FA Cup. (5.3.4)

13. Overseas player with the most appearances for United. (5.2.3)

17. Club that United competes in the "Roses Rivalry" with.

18. Romanian Club that defeated Sir Alex in his final ever Champions League group game. (3.4)

Across

3. Named captain of the women's team after the departure of Alex Greenwood. (5,5)

5. English stadium that Marcus Rashford scored his first England goal. in a friendly match against Australia. (7,2,5)

7. Last player to appear for both Manchester clubs. (4,10)

8. Centre-back who made 362 appearances for the club between 1998-2011. (3,5)

9. Was quoted in saying "I can't stand Liverpool. I can't stand the people. I can't stand anything to do with them." (4,7)

11. In 2019. Jürgen Klopp said that he might have considered signing this player had he not previously played for Manchester United. (6,11)

16. United matched their record Premier League victory in 2021 with a 9-0 victory over this opposition.

18. Second highest scoring Welshman for the club behind Ryan Giggs. (4,6)

19. Fourth top goalscorer of all-time who scored 211 goals in 424 games playing between 1937-1955. (4,6)

Down

1. First South African to play for the club. (7,7)

2. Only player to win the CONCACAF Gold Cup as a United player. (6,9)

4. French Left-back of 9 seasons at United who was one of 25 children to his parents. (7,4)

5. Birth city of Harry Maguire.

6. Striker signed on loan for the 2014/15 season from Monaco. (7,6)

10. Player that was refused a move to Liverpool against his wishes by the club in 2008. (7,6)

12. David Moyes next club after leaving United. (4,8)

13. Legendary assistant manager who the club's Young Player of the Year award is named after. (5,6)

14. First player to win the Ballon d'Or as a United player. (5,3)

15. Defender sold to Barcelona for £5 million in 2008. (6,5)

17. Metropolitan borough of Greater Manchester that United are based in.

Answers

Round 1 - Founding & History

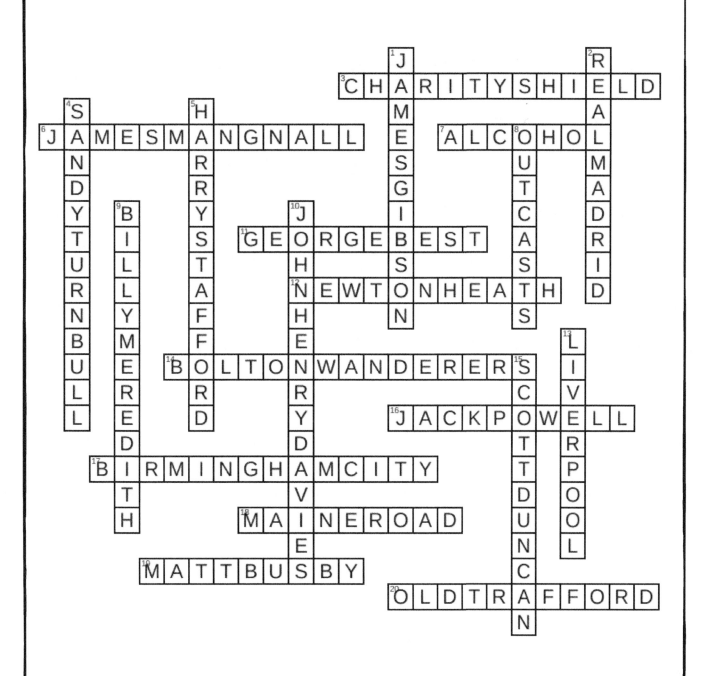

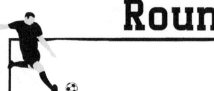

Round 2 - Old Trafford

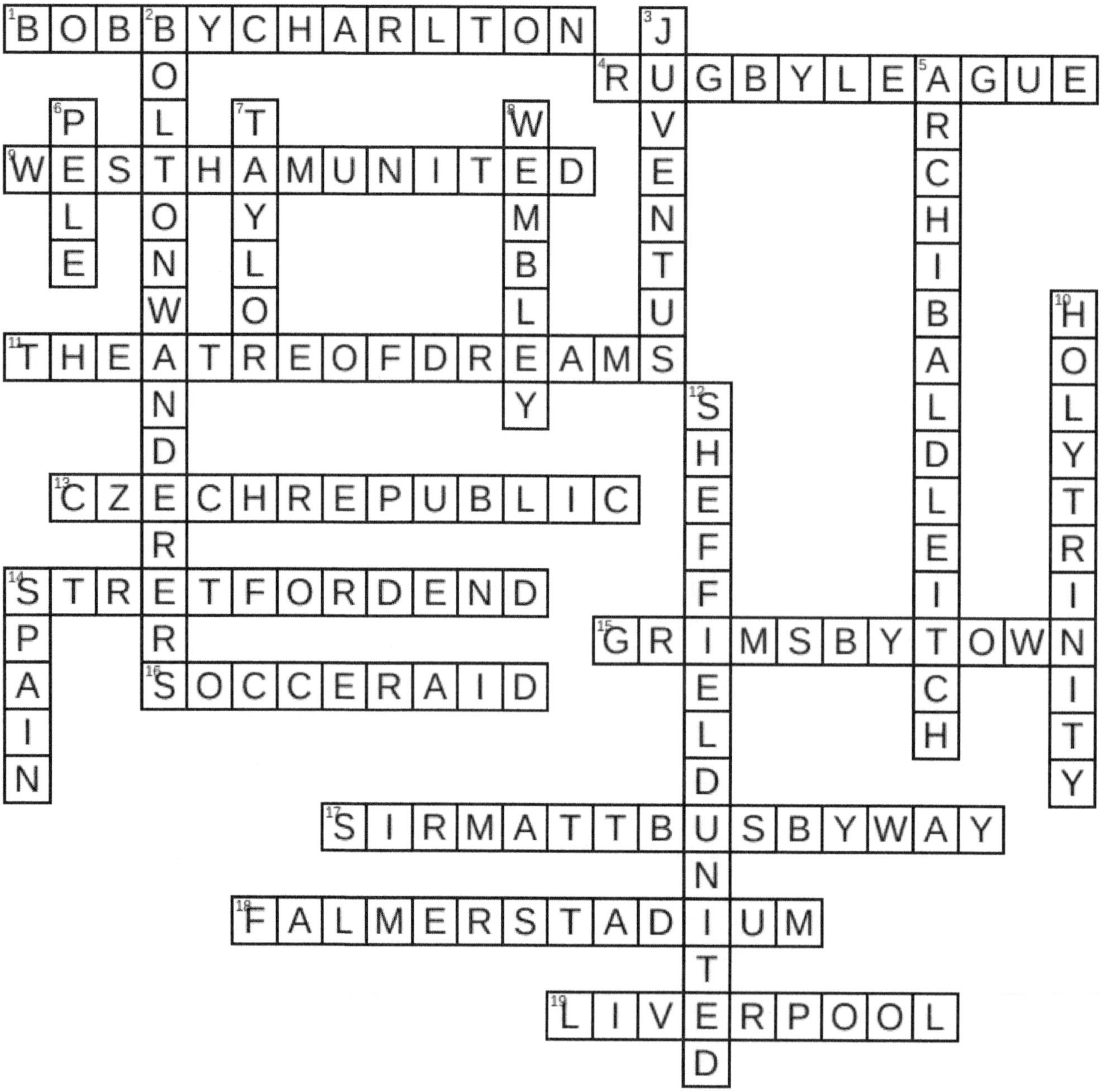
1 BOBBYCHARLTON
2 BOLTONWANDERERS
3 JUVENTUS
4 RUGBYLEAGUE
5 ARCHIBALDLEITCH
6 PELE
7 TAYLOR
8 WEMBLEY
9 WESTHAMUNITED
10 HOLYTRINITY
11 THEATREOFDREAMS
12 SHEFFIELDUNITED
13 CZECHREPUBLIC
14 STRETFORDEND
14 SPAIN
15 GRIMSBYTOWN
16 SOCCERAID
17 SIRMATTBUSBYWAY
18 FALMERSTADIUM
19 LIVERPOOL

Round 3 - Sir Matt Busby

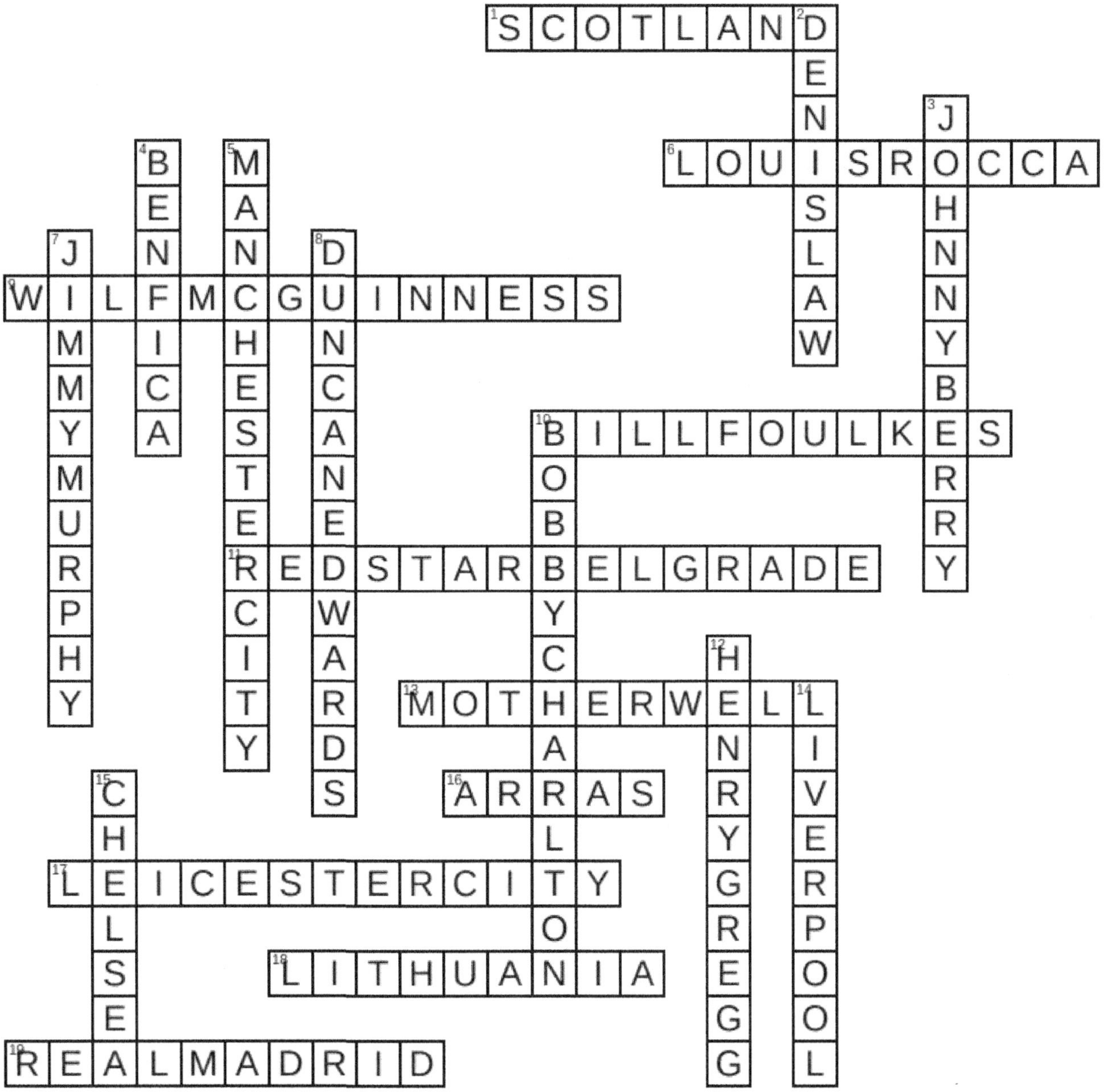

1 SCOTLAND
2 DENISLAW
3 JOHNNYBERRY
4 BENFICA
5 MANCHESTERCITY
6 LOUISROCCA
7 JIMMYMURPHY
8 DUNCANEDWARDS
9 WILFMCGUINNESS
10 BILLFOULKES
BOBBYCHARLTON
11 REDSTARBELGRADE
12 HENRYGREGG
13 MOTHERWELL
14 LIVERPOOL
15 CHELSEA
16 ARRAS
17 LEICESTERCITY
18 LITHUANIA
19 REALMADRID

Round 4 - Sir Alex Ferguson

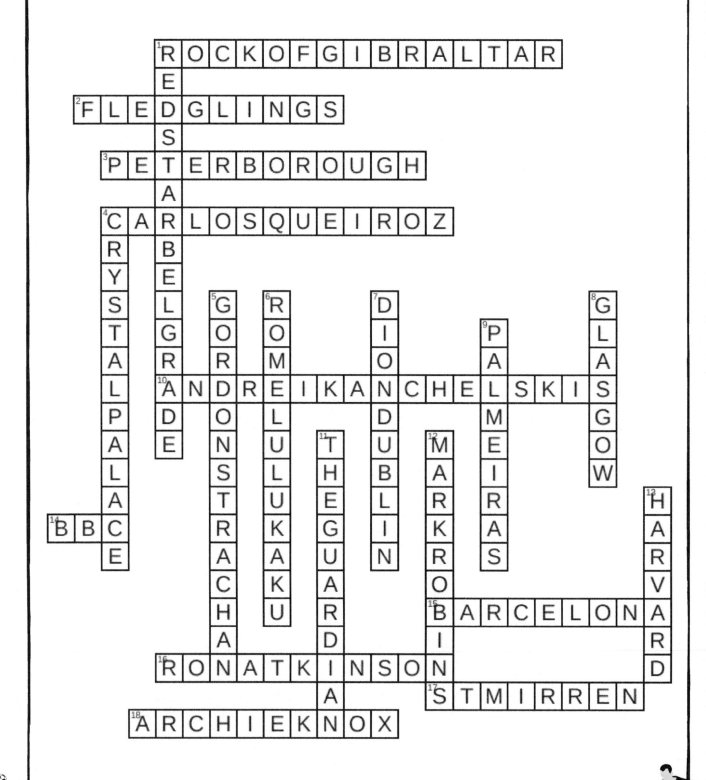

1. ROCKOFGIBRALTAR
2. FLEDGLINGS
3. PETERBOROUGH
4. CARLOSQUEIROZ
10. ANDREIKANCHELSKIS
14. BBC
15. BARCELONA
16. RONATKINSON
17. STMIRREN
18. ARCHIEKNOX

Down words:
- REDSTARBELGRADE
- CRYSTALPALACE
- GORDONSTRACHAN
- ROMELULUKAKU
- THEGUARDIAN
- DIODUBLIN
- MARKROBINS
- PALMEIRAS
- GLASGOW
- HARVARD

1 across DAVIDSADLER
2 down ARSENAL
3 down STUDIANTES
4 across PATCRERAND
5 down JOHNNYCAREY
6 across DAVIDHERD
7 down JUVENTUS
8 down BOLTONWANDERER
9 across TOMMYTAYLOR
10 across ROGERBYRNE
11 down EDDIECOLMAN
12 across MILAN
13 across JACKIEBLANCHFLOWER
14 down ITALIAN
15 down GEORGEBEST
16 across NOBBYSTILES
17 down TONYDUNNE
18 across BRIANKIDD
19 across ASTONVILLA
20 across EUSEBIO

Round 6 - 1970/80s

Round 7 - 1990s

Round 8 - 2000s

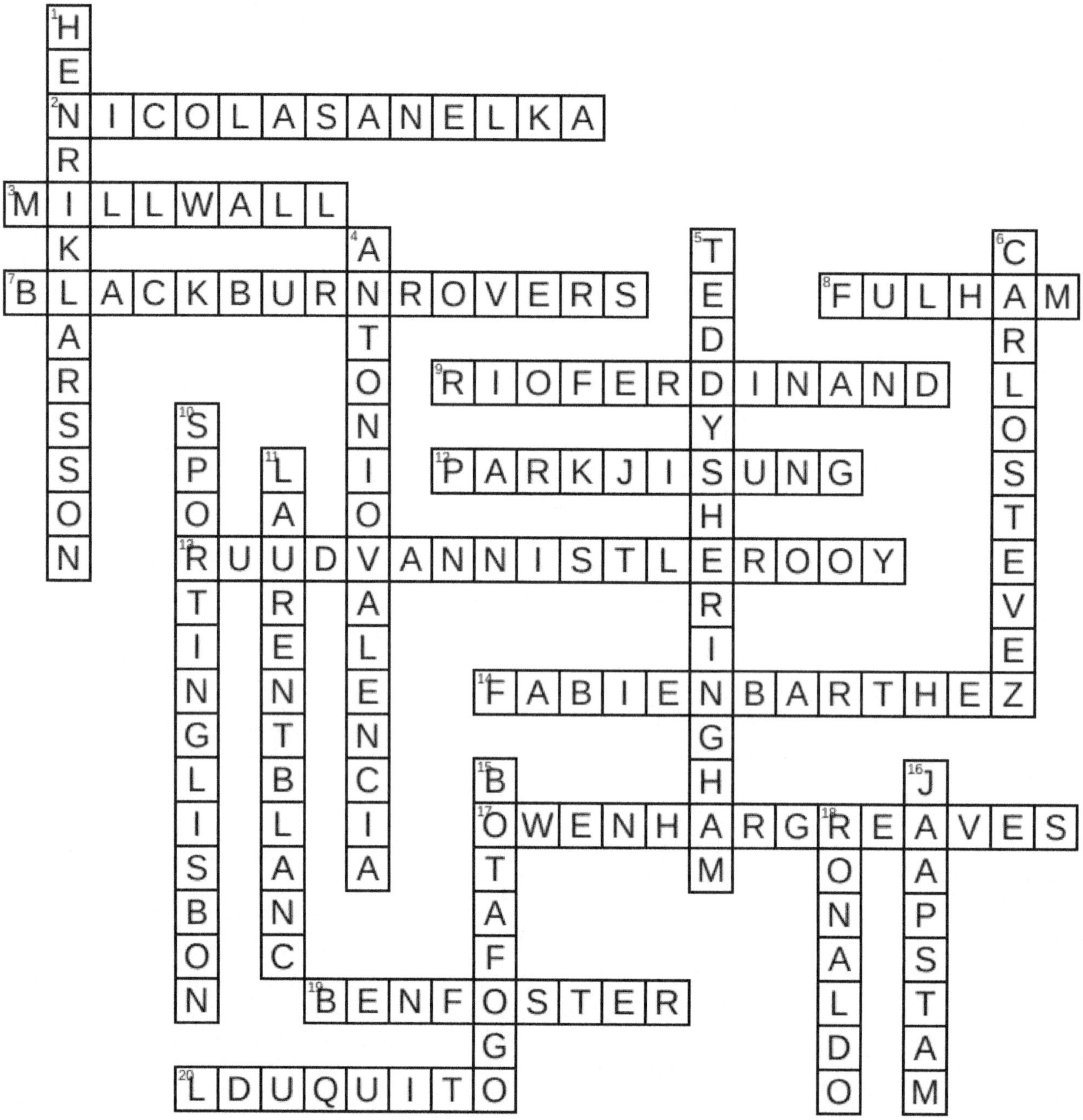
1 HENRIKLARSSON
2 NICOLASANELKA
3 MILLWALL
4 ANTONIOVALENCIA
5 TEDDYSHERINGHAM
6 CARLOSTEVEZ
7 BLACKBURNROVERS
8 FULHAM
9 RIOFERDINAND
10 SPORTINGLISBON
11 LAURENTBLANC
12 PARKJISUNG
13 RUUDVANNISTLEROOY
14 FABIENBARTHEZ
15 BOTAFOGO
16 JAAPSTAM
17 OWENHARGREAVES
18 RONALDO
19 BENFOSTER
20 LDUQUITO

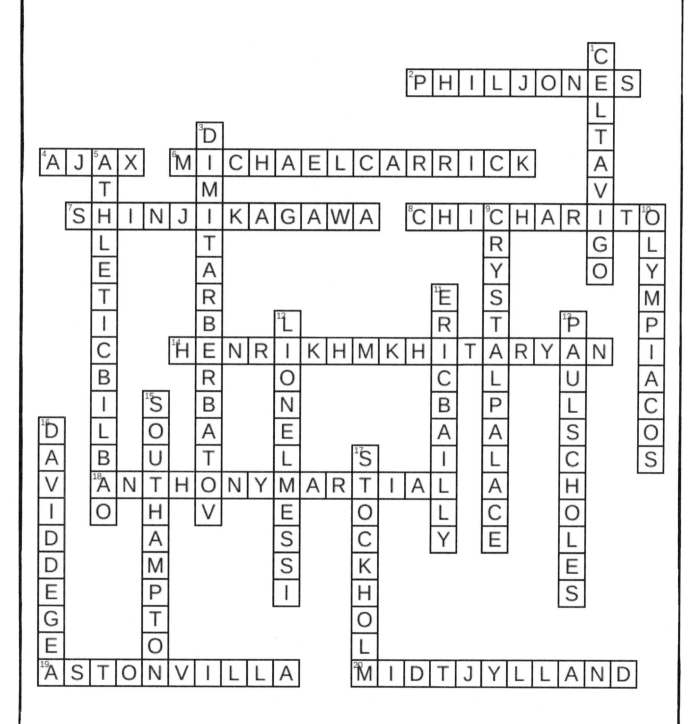

Round 9 - 2010s

Across

2. PHILJONES
4. AJAX
6. MICHAELCARRICK
7. SHINJIKAGAWA
8. CHICHARITO
14. HENRIKHMKHITARYAN
18. ANTHONYMARTIAL
19. ASTONVILLA
20. MIDTJYLLAND

Down

1. CELTAVIGO
3. DIMITARBERBATOV
5. ATHLETICBILBAO
9. CRYSTALPALACE
10. OLYMPIACOS
11. ERICBAILLY
12. LIONELMESSI
13. PAULSCHOLES
15. SOUTHAMPTON
16. DAVIDDEGEA
17. STOCKHOLM

Round 10 - Wayne Rooney

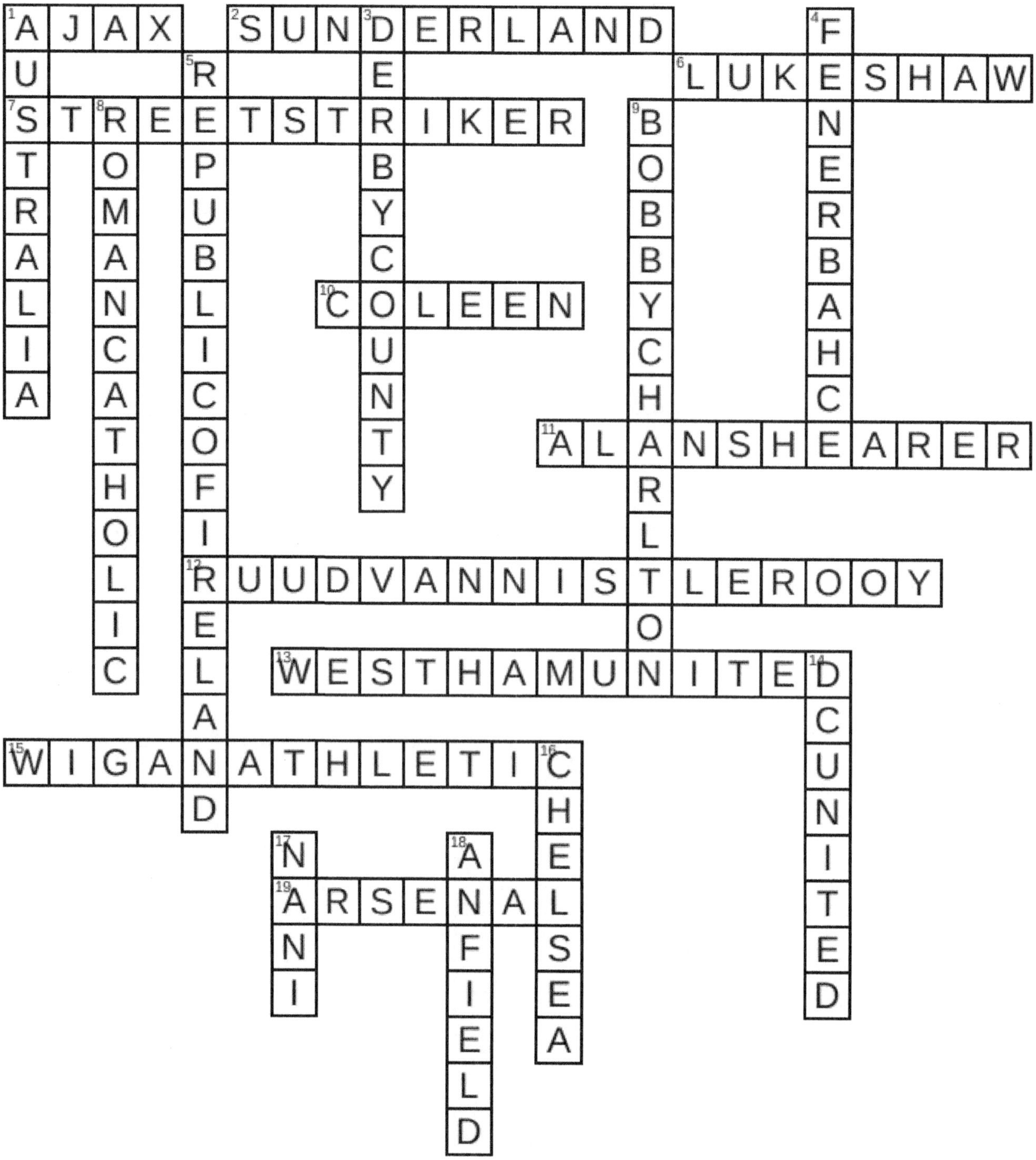

Across:
1 AJAX
2 SUNDERLAND
6 LUKESHAW
7 STREETSTRIKER
10 COLEEN
11 ALANSHEARER
12 RUUDVANNISTELROOY
13 WESTHAMUNITED
15 WIGANATHLETIC
19 ARSENAL

Down:
1 AUSTRALIA
3 DERBYCOUNTY
4 FENERBAHCE
5 REPUBLICOFIRELAND
8 ROMANCATHOLIC
9 BOBBYCHARLTON
14 DCUNITED
16 CHELSEA
17 NANI
18 ANFIELD

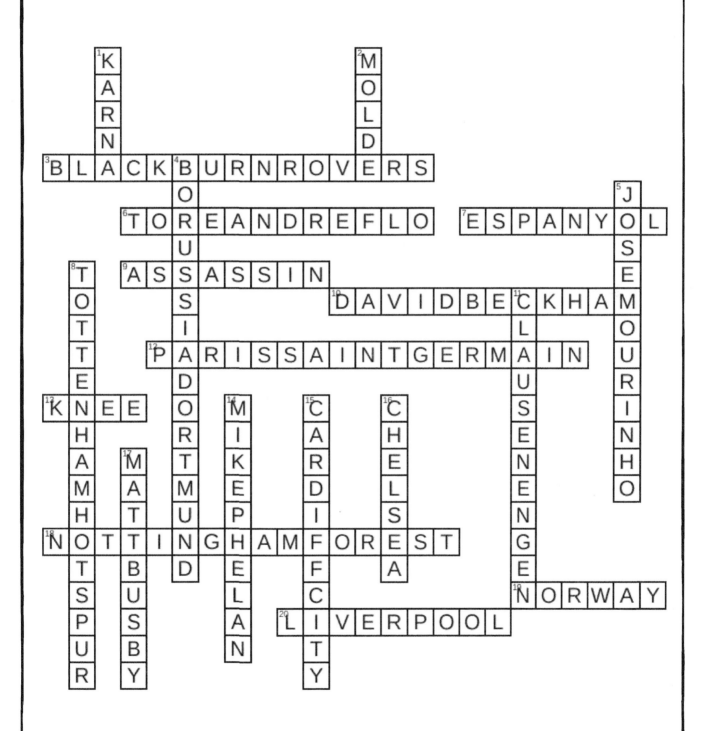

Crossword grid answers:

- INTERMIAMI
- NEVILLE
- RICHARRISON
- PHILNEVILLE
- MANCHESTERCITY
- SALFORDCITY
- PAULSCHOLES
- ALANHANSEN
- GIUSEPPEMEAZZA
- BAYERNMUNICH
- ROYKEANE
- CRYSTALPALACE
- PRESTONNORTHEND
- BURY
- RYANGIGGS
- NICKYBUTT
- DAVIDBECKHAM
- LYON
- BARCELONA
- ROBBIESAVAGE

Round 13 - Academy Graduates

1. DARREN FLETCHER
2. FRIZERCAMPBELL (FRIZERCAMPBELL)
3. ADNAN JANUZAJ
4. DANNY SIMPSON
5. TOM CLEVERLEY
6. JESSE LINGARD
7. RYAN SHAW
8. ROBBIE BRADY
9. MARCUS RASHFORD
10. DANNY WELBECK
11. SCOTT MCTOMINAY
12. MICHAEL KEANE
13. PHIL BARDSLEY
14. FEDERICO MACHEDA
15. JONNY EVANS
16. JOSH KING
17. PAUL POGBA
18. MASON GREENWOOD
19. RAFAEL
20. RAVEL MORRISON

Round 14 - Club Captains

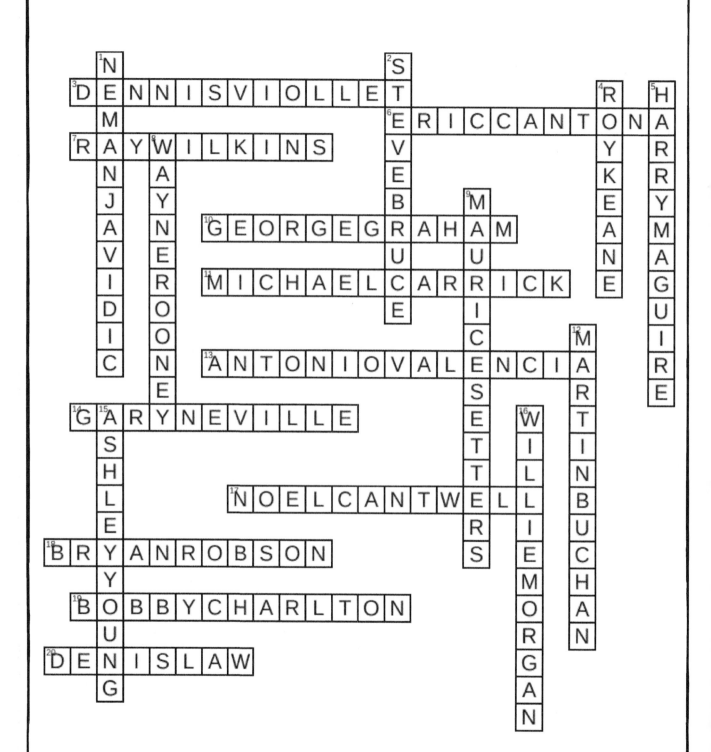

1 N
3 DENNISVIOLLET
2 S
4 R
5 H
6 ERICCANTONA
7 RAYWILKINS
9 M
10 GEORGEGRAHAM
11 MICHAELCARRICK
12 M
13 ANTONIOVALENCIA
14 GARYNEVILLE
15 A
16 W
17 NOELCANTWELL
18 BRYANROBSON
19 BOBBYCHARLTON
20 DENISLAW

Round 15 - Cristiano Ronaldo

Round 16 - Roy Keane

Crossword grid answers:

Across:
- 2. JASONMCATEER
- 5. MAURICE
- 8. ALFINGEHÅLAND
- 9. MICKMCCARTHY
- 10. SHEFFIELDUNITED
- 14. PRAWNSANDWICHBRIGADE
- 17. CORK
- 18. CARLOSQUEIROZ
- 19. SOUTHAMPTON
- 20. LUISGARCIA

Down:
- 1. NOTTINGHAMFOREST
- 3. CELTIC
- 4. JUVENTUS
- 6. MIDDLESBROUGH
- 7. BLACKBURNROVER
- 11. TRIGGS
- 12. SUNDERLAND
- 13. PATRICKVIEIRA
- 15. ERICCANTONA
- 16. GRAHAMCAMPBELL

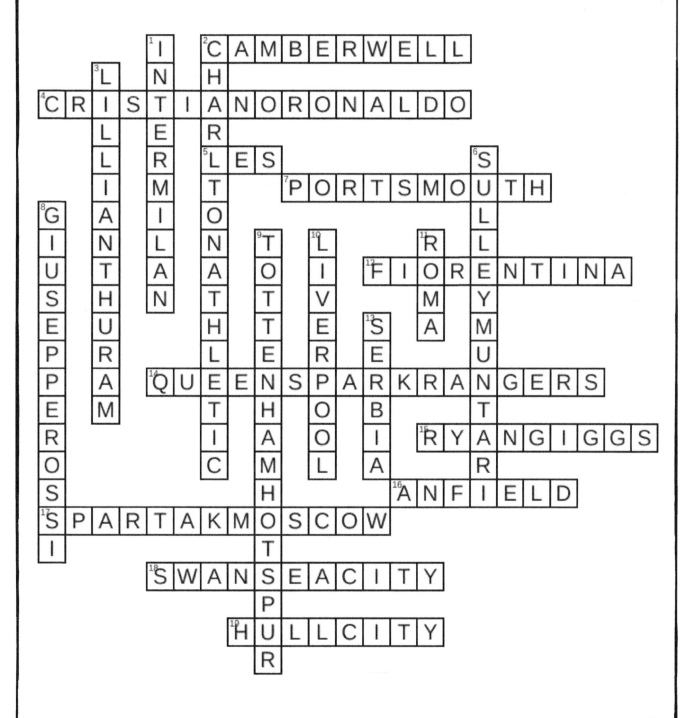

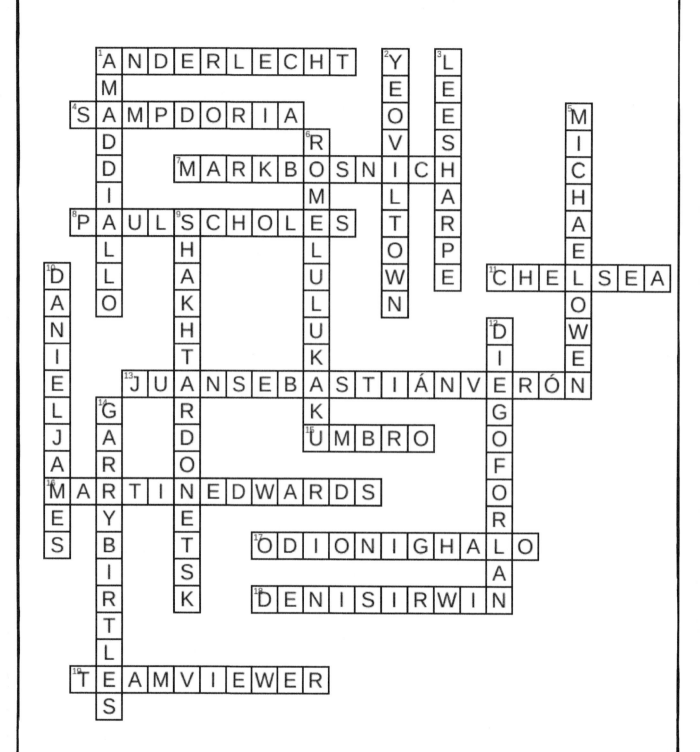

Across/Down grid entries:

1. ANDERLECHT
2. YEOVILTOWN
3. LEESHARPE
4. SAMPDORIA
5. MICHAELOWEN
6. ROMELULUKAKU
7. MARKBOSNICH
8. PAULSCHOLES
9. SHAKHTARDONETSK
10. DANIELJAMES
11. CHELSEA
12. DIEGOFORLAN
13. JUANSEBASTIÁNVERÓN
14. GARYBIRTLES
15. UMBRO
16. MARTINEDWARDS
17. ODIONIGHALO
18. DENISIRWIN
19. TEAMVIEWER

AMADDIDIALLO

Round 19 - General II

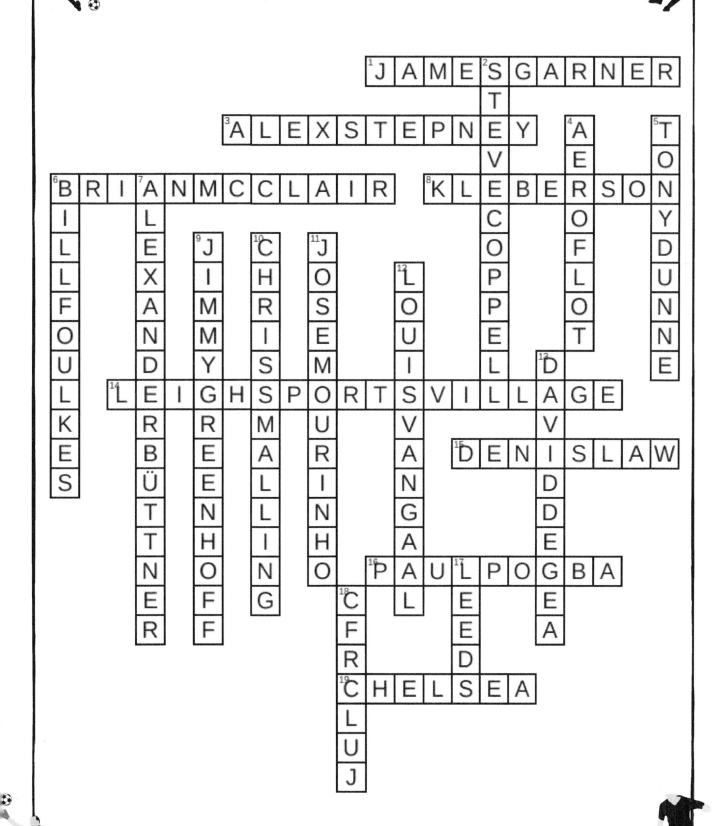

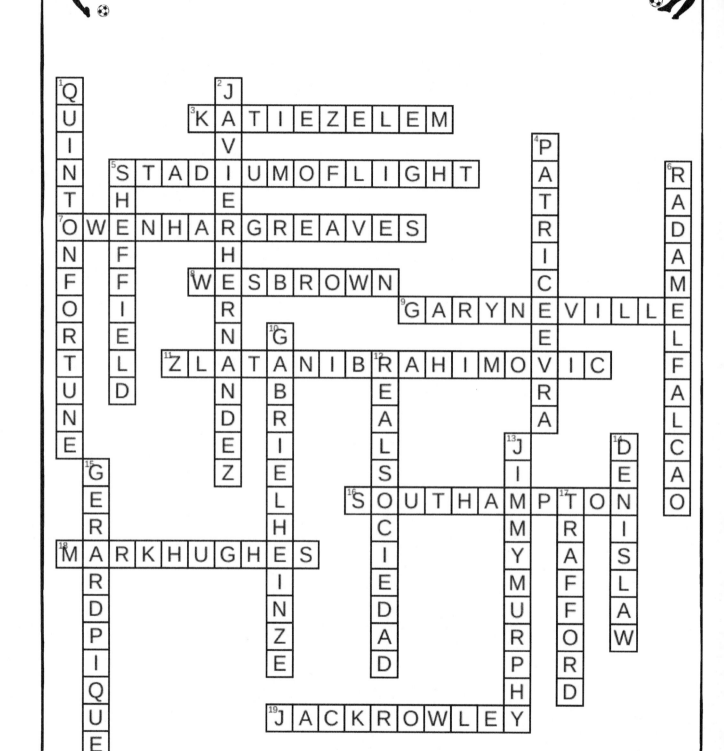

Crossword grid answers:

3. KATIEZELEM
5. STADIUMOFLIGHT
7. OWENHARGREAVES
8. WESBROWN
9. GARYNEVILLE
11. ZLATANIBRAHIMOVIC
16. SOUTHAMPTON
18. MARKHUGHES
19. JACKROWLEY

Down:
1. QUINTONFORTUNE
2. JAVIERHERNANDEZ
4. PATRICEEVRA
5. SHEFFIELD
6. RADAMELFALCAO
10. GABRIELHEINZE
12. REALSOCIEDAD
13. JIMMYMURPHY
14. DENISLAW
15. GERARDPIQUE
17. TRAFFORD

That's all folks. thank you so much for purchasing this Manchester United crossword book. I really hope you enjoyed it and learnt some cool facts about the club to impress your fellow red devils.

As a small independent publisher any reviews you can leave will be a big help as I try to grow my company and produce better and better books for you to enjoy.

If you have any criticisms please do email me before leaving a negative review and I'd be happy to assist you if you have any problems!

kieran.brown2402@gmail.com

Printed in Great Britain
by Amazon